WHO WERE THE

ROMANS?

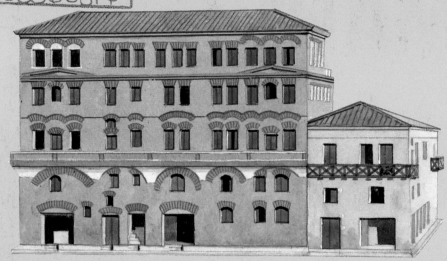

First published in 2006
in the UK by Franklin Watts
338 Euston Road, London NW1 3BH

Franklin Watts Australia, Hachette Children's Books
Level 17/207 Kent Street, Sydney NSW 2000

This series was devised and produced by McRae Books Srl,
Borgo S. Croce, 8, Florence (Italy)
Publishers: Anne McRae and Marco Nardi
Text: Loredana Agosta
Main Illustrations: Lorenzo Cecchi, Luisa Della Porta,
Inklink, Alessandro Menchi, MM comunicazione
(Manuela Cappon, Monica Favilli), Paola Ravaglia
Illustrations: Studio Stalio (Alessandro Cantucci,
Fabiano Fabbrucci, Margherita Salvadori)
Design: Marco Nardi

Colour separations: Fotolito Toscana, Firenze

A CIP catalogue record for this book is available
from the British Library.
Dewey Decimal Classification Number: 937

ISBN 0 7496 6791 5
ISBN-13 978 0 7496 6791 7

Printed and bound in Italy.

WHO WERE THE
ROMANS?

W

FRANKLIN WATTS
LONDON • SYDNEY

Religion
see pages 12-13

Food
see page 24

The
Ancient Roman World

■ The Roman Empire at
its greatest extent

BRITANNIA

Londinium •

GAUL

HISPANIA

ITALY

• Rome

Carthage •

GREECE

Athens •

MEDITERRANEAN SEA

BLACK SEA

• Constantinople

ANATOLIA

• Ephesus

NORTH
AFRICA

• Alexandria

World Map

Warships
see page 18

Trade and Transport
see pages 14-15

Warriors and War
see pages 18-19

Contents

The Roman Empire
see pages 10-11

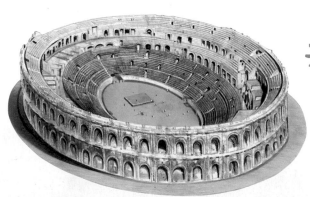

 Feast Days and Fun in Ancient Rome
see pages 16-17

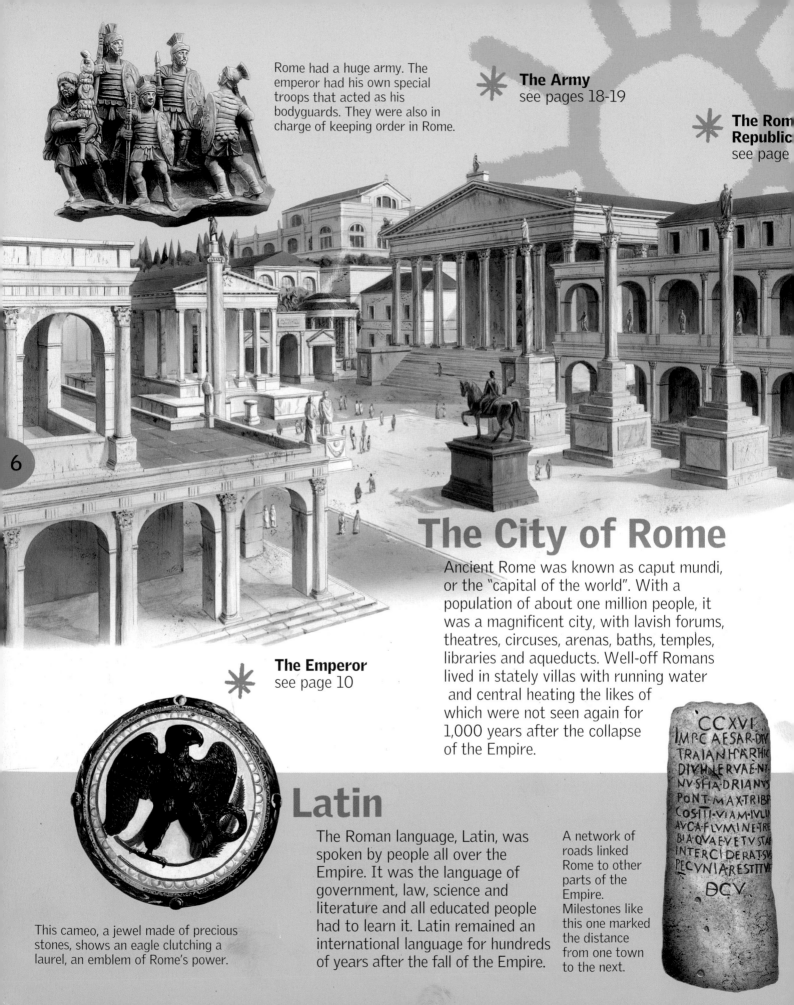

Rome had a huge army. The emperor had his own special troops that acted as his bodyguards. They were also in charge of keeping order in Rome.

The Army
see pages 18-19

The Rom
Republic
see page

6

The City of Rome

Ancient Rome was known as caput mundi, or the "capital of the world". With a population of about one million people, it was a magnificent city, with lavish forums, theatres, circuses, arenas, baths, temples, libraries and aqueducts. Well-off Romans lived in stately villas with running water and central heating the likes of which were not seen again for 1,000 years after the collapse of the Empire.

The Emperor
see page 10

Latin

The Roman language, Latin, was spoken by people all over the Empire. It was the language of government, law, science and literature and all educated people had to learn it. Latin remained an international language for hundreds of years after the fall of the Empire.

A network of roads linked Rome to other parts of the Empire. Milestones like this one marked the distance from one town to the next.

This cameo, a jewel made of precious stones, shows an eagle clutching a laurel, an emblem of Rome's power.

Law

In 450 BC the Romans wrote one of the first legal codes, setting down laws that magistrates had to follow regardless of who they were judging. Almost 1,000 years later, the Emperor Justinian set down legal codes that form the basis of much modern European law.

Technology

The Romans were master engineers and builders and they brought their advanced technology to all the areas they conquered. The roads and bridges they built made long-distance travel fast and efficient, while their huge aqueducts carried clean water to towns.

Pipes beneath city streets carried fresh water to Roman houses.

 Water Supply see page 23

Who were the Ancient Romans?

The Romans were a group of Italian people who began to conquer a vast empire about 2,500 years ago. From the city of Rome, they first took control of Italy and then gradually spread into the Middle East, North Africa and many parts of Europe. Wherever they conquered they also settled, teaching the locals Roman ways and also adopting many of the local customs. In this way they built an international civilization that lasted for over 1,000 years.

Marcus Aurelius, one of the best-loved emperors, was also one of Rome's great thinkers.

 Education see page 29

Literature

The 1st century BC was a golden age of Latin literature. Virgil was one of the most important writers and he wrote the Aeneid, an epic poem about the founding of Rome. Roman literature is still studied today.

There were many libraries in ancient Roman cities. This one stood at Ephesus.

7

Timeline

The ancient Roman civilization lasted for more than 1,000 years. This timeline shows some of the main events or periods in Roman history.

Villages on the Palatine Hills gradually join together to form the city of Rome
1000 BC

Etruscan kings rule Rome
625-510 BC

The Roman Republic
509-31 BC

First Roman Emperor
31 BC

Constantinople becomes the capital of the Empire AD 330

The Empire is divided
AD 395

The Western Empire falls
AD 476

8

This stone was carved with an early form of Latin, the language of the Romans.

The Etruscans

Along with the Greeks in the south, the Etruscans were the most advanced people in Italy. Their civilization reached its peak about 600 BC. The Etruscans greatly influenced the Romans on matters ranging from technology to art and religion.

The head of a goddess crafted in Rome by Etruscan craftspeople.

The Origins
of Rome

Roman civilization was based on the city of Rome, in central Italy. It was here that the first simple villages were founded. They gradually became linked to form a single city. At first, Rome was governed by a monarchy of Etruscan kings until they were expelled from the city in 509 BC. Then, for almost 500 years, Rome became a republic, and was ruled by an elected government chosen from the wealthiest families.

Remus and Romulus

According to legend, the city of Rome was founded by the twin brothers Remus and Romulus. Their mother was forced to abandon them as babies. The twins, however, were saved by a she-wolf who nursed them and by shepherds who raised them. When the twins grew up, they founded the city and fought over who should rule it. Romulus killed Remus and the city took his name.

This head of a she-wolf is a detail of a bronze sculpture made by Etruscan artists.

The Roman Republic

The Republic was founded after the last Etruscan king was defeated. Roman citizens were free to elect their own leaders to govern Rome, make laws, handle finances and carry out the construction of important buildings. The 500 years of the Republic were turbulent and violent times, during which the Romans greatly expanded their territories.

A bronze statue of an Etruscan warrior.

The Senate meetings took place at a temple called the Curia. Before each meeting, prayers were recited and sacrificial offerings made.

A portrait bust of Lucius Junius Brutus, one of the founders of the Republic.

9

The Senate

The two most powerful people, the Consuls, were elected from a group called the Senate. Initially only the wealthiest nobles could join the Senate, but later the number was increased and ordinary citizens were allowed to join. In imperial times the Senate lost most of its power to the emperors.

This coin shows a Roman citizen casting his vote.

The First Emperor

The Roman Republic came to an end when Octavian, a mighty general and the adopted son of Julius Caesar, became Emperor Augustus. Although the Emperor shared some of his powers with the Senate, he had complete control. The Emperor divided the Empire into provinces and appointed trusted officials to govern them.

This statue of Emperor Augustus shows him in military dress and his arm raised to address his subjects.

This Roman statue represents Victory.

The Roman Empire

The Roman Empire reached it maximum size under the great military leader, Emperor Trajan (ruled AD 98-117). At that time it stretched from modern-day Iraq to England, and from North Africa to Germany. About 50 million people lived within its borders. Soldiers sent to enforce Roman law in the conquered lands settled there, introducing the Roman way of life, from baths and amphitheatres, to good roads and water supply.

When the Romans took over a territory, they began to build roads, baths, government buildings and other structures necessary for the proper management of the colony.

Colonies

The Romans began to conquer and take possession of neighbouring lands during the time of the Republic. When the Empire was established, their expansion continued. The people living in these territories under the control of Rome, known as the provinces, were forced to pay taxes and follow Roman law.

The Empire was at its greatest extent during the rule of Emperor Trajan, who made Mesopotamia a Roman province.

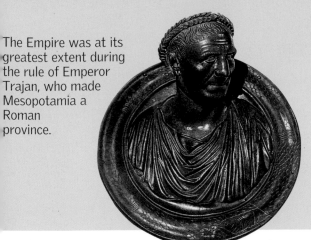

East and West

For the first 200 years the Roman Empire was peaceful and stable. Then came a period of almost a century of civil war and constant attack from abroad. The Empire was much weakened. In 284 Emperor Diocletian divided it into the Eastern Empire and the Western Empire. Later, in 324, Constantine reunited it and then moved the capital from Rome to Constantinople. But this unity did not last and in 395 the Empire was divided once more.

Emperor Hadrian built a wall across Britain to mark the northern border of the Empire and to protect it from raids by the wild tribes to the north.

The Fall

From around AD 200, more and more Germanic tribes began to raid the Empire. Many of them settled within the frontiers and some even became Roman soldiers. By the early 5th century foreign raiders were pouring through the borders in numbers that the Romans were unable to turn back or absorb. Rome was sacked by the Visigoths in 410 and the Western Empire fell to the invaders in 476.

The divided Empire was ruled by four men called tetrarchs. Each part of the Empire was ruled by a supreme leader, called Augustus, and his second-in-command, called Caesar.

11

Jupiter was identified with the Greek god Zeus.

Gods and Goddesses

The ancient Romans adopted many gods and goddesses from the ancient Greeks and from other peoples they conquered. The chief god was Jupiter, the patron of the state. The great temple on Capitol Hill was built to honour him and his companion goddesses, Juno (queen of the gods) and Minerva (goddess of warriors, wisdom and crafts).

This rattle, called a sistrum, was used during worship of the Egyptian goddess Isis, one of the many foreign goddesses absorbed into Roman religion.

A reconstruction of the Temple of Palestrina, the largest temple in Republican times, dedicated to the goddess Fortuna.

Temples

Temples were considered the dwelling places of the gods. A huge statue of the god or goddess to whom the temple was dedicated stood inside each one. The statue faced the entrance where an altar stood, upon which worshippers performed sacrifices.

Fortuna, the Roman goddess of luck, was worshipped so that she could help people in various moments of their lives.

In this carving, animals are led to a temple altar in preparation for sacrifice.

Offerings

Public ceremonies and rituals were a big part of Roman religion. Worshippers made offerings of wine, milk, honey and incense, and made animal sacrifices of pigs, sheep or oxen. When an animal was slaughtered its internal organs were offered to the gods while the rest was eaten at special banquets.

The Lares

The Romans believed that household spirits and minor gods, called penates and lares, dwelled in and guarded the home. Every home had an altar where offerings were made every day.

The painting on this household shrine shows a god specially venerated by a family, flanked by two lares.

Religion

The Romans worshipped many gods and goddesses. Some were native Roman gods while others were borrowed from the Greeks and Etruscans. As the Empire grew, new cults were introduced from many different lands. Public religion was generally formal while private worship included the veneration of household spirits and ancestors.

Vestal Virgins

To ensure the prosperity of Rome, the flame of Vesta, goddess of the hearth, had to be kept alive. Priestesses, called the Vestal Virgins, were entrusted with this task. They were chosen at a young age from among Rome's noble families to guard the flame which burned in Vesta's shrine, located in the forum.

The flame had to burn continuously, day and night. According to ancient Roman belief, if the flame went out, Rome would be doomed.

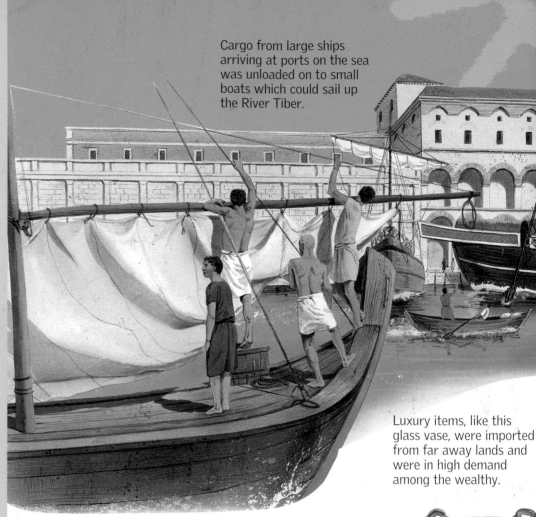

Scales like this one were used to weigh items before they were bought or sold.

Cargo from large ships arriving at ports on the sea was unloaded on to small boats which could sail up the River Tiber.

Weights

The Romans developed a standard for measuring weight based on the Greek system. Their standard, an object used to compare other items, was kept in the Temple of Jupiter on Capitol Hill. To prevent merchants from cheating their customers, there was tight control over weighing procedures.

Trajan's market had 150 shops on four levels – just like a modern shopping mall.

Luxury items, like this glass vase, were imported from far away lands and were in high demand among the wealthy.

At Sea

Shipping goods by sea was by far the best method. Merchant ships came in many shapes and sizes. Some ships, designed to transport barrels of wine, olive oil and sacks of grain, could carry over 250 tonnes. Merchants usually sailed close to the coast and made numerous stops along the way, stopping at ports to rest for the night. The port at Ostia, at the mouth of the Tiber, became the main centre for business.

Merchants

By law, members of the Senate were not allowed to conduct business. Most merchants came from the wealthy group of the upper class known as Equestrians. Some were like bankers, lending money and holding deposits. Other merchants, including shopkeepers and sellers in open-air markets, were from the lower classes.

Trade

Different metals, like gold, silver, and bronze, were used to make coins. Although coins of high value were minted only in Rome, coins of lesser value, used for everyday purchases, were minted in various cities of the Empire. Provincial coins were made for local use. A common currency made trading easier.

Designs on coins featured the portraits of emperors, the gods or important events.

Rome and other cities had to import large amounts of food, oil, wine, wool and other basic necessities. Wealthy Romans expected to find luxury goods, such as incense, spices and silk, in their markets and these were brought from distant lands. The Romans established a coinage system within the Empire which made trading much easier.

Donkeys, mules and oxen were used by traders and travellers. Animals were fed or exchanged at rest stops along the road.

Travel

The network of roads which linked Rome to most of its provinces was originally built by the army as they gradually extended the boundaries of the Empire. Merchants, messengers and travellers also used the roads. Transporting goods by land however was slow, expensive and dangerous and merchandise was mainly moved by boat.

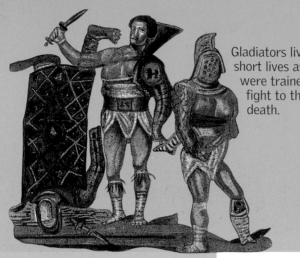

Gladiators lived short lives as they were trained to fight to the death.

Gladiators

The most famous of all Roman entertainers were the gladiators. They entered the arena to face other gladiators or ferocious animals. Gladiators were usually slaves or prisoners who were bought and sold and forced to compete. A few people chose to make their living as gladiators, enjoying the fame and the prize money.

Feast Days
and Fun

All sorts of exotic animals were imported for the entertainment of the crowds.

To win favour, emperors spent large sums of money to provide free food and entertainment for the masses. Romans were entertained by violent and bloody performances, such as the torture of animals and execution of criminals. In private, wealthy citizens indulged in lavish feasts. Music and dancing accompanied the celebration of the various feast days set aside to honour the gods.

Arenas, like this one in southern France, are called amphitheatres. Thanks to the genius of Roman architects, many still stand today.

Amphitheatres

Almost every Roman town had an amphitheatre, or arena. Some were quite large, with seating for thousands of spectators. The finest arenas, like the Colosseum in Rome, had an understage, where a system of trap doors and elevators brought both beasts and gladiators up to the stage.

Spectators used tickets like these to enter arenas. Special entrances were reserved for the upper classes

Festivals

The Roman calendar had many feast days and festivals to honour the gods. Some were reserved for formal ceremonies while others included wild merry-making, music and dance. One of the most important festivals, Saturnalia, took place in December and honoured Saturn, the god of agriculture.

This inscription of a Roman calendar shows the months written across the top while the days of the week are marked with letters running from top to bottom.

Great banquets were held during Saturnalia, an occasion when the rules were broken and slaves were served by their masters.

Banquets

Wealthy Romans, like the Etruscans, enjoyed their meals lying down on couches arranged around a low table. Banquets lasted for hours and included many courses starting with seafood and eggs, then roasted meats and vegetables, and ending with fruits and nuts. There was always plenty of wine on hand.

Theatre

Theatrical performances were popular in Rome. Both tragedies and comedies, many based on Greek plays, were performed. The Romans also enjoyed light-hearted entertainment, and clowns and mimes often stole the show.

Actors wore masks like these, with emphasised facial expressions so that the characters they played could be recognised by everyone, even those seated at the back.

In battle, Romans used tall structures called siege towers to knock down city walls. The lower level had a battering ram for heavy blows. Archers were stationed at the top.

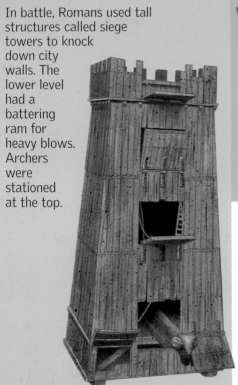

Wars

Some of the most noteworthy feats of the Roman army date back to Republican times. The Punic Wars, fought against Carthage (in North Africa), lasted for over a century and ended with the total destruction of Carthage.

The Carthaginians used elephants to invade Italy. These huge powerful beasts terrified Roman troops. Later, the Romans would also use elephants and they often played a decisive role in battle.

Tactics

Army generals planned battles well in advance and waited for the right moment to launch their attack. At times the army never engaged in battle, but instead set up camps just outside enemy territory and waited for weeks or months, for the enemy to surrender or starve to death.

Warships were powered by rows of oars.

Warships

Many important battles were also fought at sea. Emperor Augustus did a lot to strengthen the navy Huge warships carried soldiers to the Mediterranean and Black seas to defend Roman ports and waterways. The navy also hunted down and captured pirates who threatened trading ships loaded with precious cargo.

The Roman army had to defend the Empire from invasion. Raiding armies of Germanic tribes posed a constant threat and ultimately contributed to the fall of the Western Empire.

Each legion carried a standard – a decorated pole – into battle. They were not only symbols of honour but were also used to send signals to soldiers in battle.

Soldiers wore metal helmets, breastplates, and chin guards and carried huge shields to protect themselves.

Warriors
and War

The army was the basis of the Roman Empire. It was well-organised, disciplined and armed with the most advanced weapons of its day. Roman generals were both respected and feared. Apart from fighting to extend Roman territory, soldiers also had to defend frontiers and fend off invasion. Over the course of the centuries this proved to be a difficult and, in the end, impossible undertaking and the great Roman Empire fell to foreign invaders.

The Army

The Roman army was the first in history to be made up almost entirely of professional, volunteer soldiers. Armies were divided up into units called legions, which were further divided into cohorts and centuries. Each century had its own leader, or centurion. Foot soldiers and horsemen were trained for all kinds of battle.

Weapons

Legionaries carried swords and spears for one-on-one combat. They were also armed with heavy javelins which would break upon impact so that they could not be used by the enemy. Technology also played a great part in the success of the Roman army. Various kinds of machines, like catapults, were made to hurl heavy stones at enemy defences.

The onager, shown here, was the most powerful machine. It was named after the Persian wild ass, because of its forceful kick.

Mosaics were either bright and colourful, like the one shown here, or done in clear cut black and white. Some mosaics showed patterns while others had life-like scenes.

Mosaics

Walls, floors and ceilings were decorated with designs created by fitting together small pieces of coloured glass and stone. These works are called mosaics. Skilled artists were able to achieve brilliant effects and create life-like images.

Painting

Painters in Roman times made paint by mixing hot beeswax and pigments. Walls in the homes of the wealthy were decorated with frescoes. They depicted landscapes, still-lifes, and scenes from everyday life and mythology. Portraits were also popular subjects.

Many paintings, like this one of a young woman holding a type of pen and wooden writing tablets, were found in the city of Pompeii (southern Italy).

Art
and Architecture

Most Roman art was created to commemorate military victories and to glorify gods and public figures or heroes. Art was made for private places too, enriching the homes of the wealthy. Although Roman artists were inspired by the Greeks and Etruscans, they developed their own style which spread throughout the Empire.

Sculpture

Roman sculptors owed much to their Greek predecessors. However, their sculptures, especially the portraits of shrewd businessmen and military leaders, were often telling snapshots of the ruthless men who ran the Empire.

This tomb, carved for a member of the imperial family, was made from porphyry stone

Monuments

Many monuments, such as triumphal arches, were erected in the forum. Emperors returning from war would pass through the arches in victory marches, parading their booty and captives. The arches were decorated with carvings illustrating heroic deeds.

The triumphal arch of Constantine was built to commemorate the Emperor's victory over his rival, Maxentius.

The gigantic baths complexes gave architects the opportunity to show their many skills, both of a practical and artistic nature. This cutaway of the Baths of Caracalla shows the many rooms. The baths could accommodate 1,600 bathers and covered almost 1.5 square km.

The basic plan for Roman temples was borrowed from the ancient Greeks. Temples were built on high platforms and were surrounded by rows of columns.

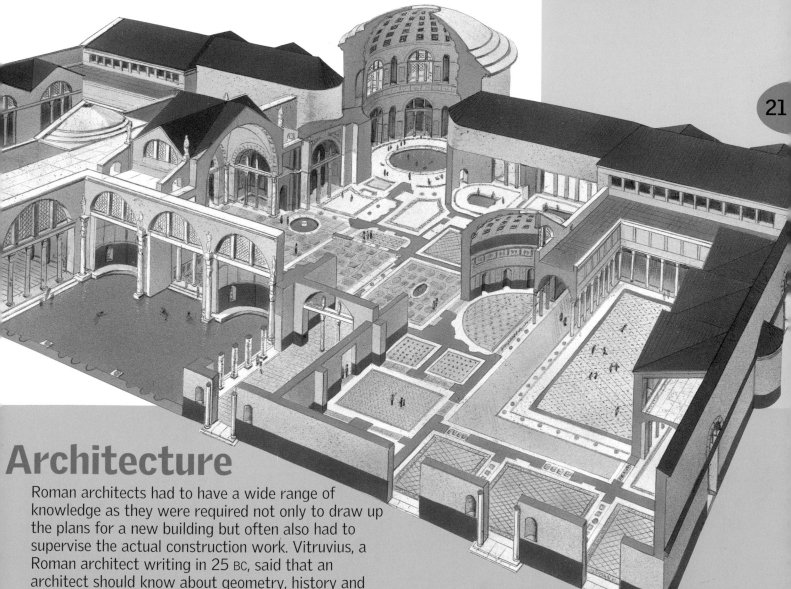

Architecture

Roman architects had to have a wide range of knowledge as they were required not only to draw up the plans for a new building but often also had to supervise the actual construction work. Vitruvius, a Roman architect writing in 25 BC, said that an architect should know about geometry, history and music, as well as medicine, astrology and cosmology.

The Arch

Roman engineers developed the arch which allowed them to span wide spaces with their bridges and aqueducts.

The Milvian Bridge in Rome, which crosses the River Tiber, was built over 2,000 years ago and still stands today.

Science and Technology

The Romans excelled in practical matters, such as building roads, bridges and drains, and in making machines and tools. At first their knowledge came from the ancient Greeks, but they quickly surpassed them. They applied their skills to projects large and small; from the vast network of roads that linked every part of the Empire to the manufacture of small items in clay and glass.

In this detail from a wall painting, a doctor extracts an arrow from a soldier's thigh.

Medicine

Almost all Roman doctors received their training in Greece and many Greek doctors practiced in Rome. Doctors performed operations and used all sorts of herbs and plants and special diets to cure illness. Hospitals were founded to treat soldiers wounded in battle.

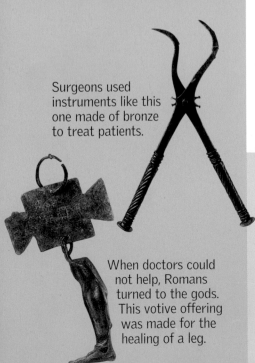

Surgeons used instruments like this one made of bronze to treat patients.

When doctors could not help, Romans turned to the gods. This votive offering was made for the healing of a leg.

Machines

The Romans used slave and animal labour in many of their building projects. They also devised clever machines to lift heavy weights, like the one shown here. A large winch was powered by slaves treading the big wheel at the bottom.

Water Works

The Roman water system was better than any others built in Europe before the 19th century. Aqueducts, both below and above ground, brought fresh water into baths, wealthy homes and city wells. Underground drains removed sewage, keeping cities clean and preventing disease.

Roman workers building an arched bridge aqueduct.

Roads

Road builders (usually soldiers) began by marking out parallel tracks and then digging down between them until they reached a solid foundation. They filled this trench with layers of sand, lime, clay, stones and fragments of terracotta. On top, they laid wide flint or lava stones to create a smooth surface.

Roman roads laid 2,000 years ago are still intact in many parts of Europe.

The Romans were skilled glassmakers. They made ornate bowls for show, but also practical glass bottles and tumblers that were used in everyday life.

Terracotta jars, called amphorae, were used to store oil and wine.

Food

Romans ate a wide range of vegetables, cereals and fruit. They drank milk and ate cheese made from ewe's, goat's and cow's milk. They flavoured their foods with many different herbs and spices. Meat and fish were also common foods although most people could not afford to eat them everyday.

This detail from a wall painting shows a glass bowl overflowing with apples, grapes and pomegranates.

Daily Life

Lifestyles varied greatly in Roman times, depending on how rich or poor people were and whether they lived in a great city like Rome, or in the countryside of the far-flung provinces. Daily life in Rome itself was bustling, busy, noisy and probably quite dirty too. The city streets were crowded with merchants, slaves, off-duty soldiers, pilgrims and visitors of every kind and the air was filled with the cries of shopkeepers and hawkers flogging their wares.

Storage

Before refrigerators, keeping food fresh was a problem. Many people had cool cellars or pantries in their homes for food storage. Others probably used lots of strong herbs and spices to disguise the bad taste of food that had gone off.

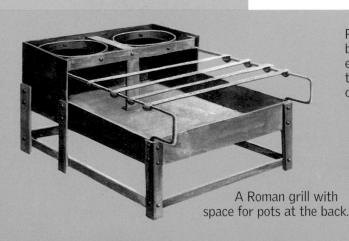

A Roman grill with space for pots at the back.

Pans like this may have been used to cook eggs or to bake things in the oven.

Cooking

Many Roman homes did not have kitchens. Some people ate in taverns, although most bought cooked food from street stalls or taverns and took it home with them to eat. The rich had well-equipped kitchens with slaves to cook and serve their food.

Apartment Blocks

Most city-dwellers lived in apartment blocks that stood up to six storeys tall. The ground floor was generally taken up with shops and warehouses that opened onto the street. The apartments above were often small and cramped. They were also cold since the windows had no glass and there was no heating.

Many apartment blocks were poorly built and they often collapsed. Fires were another constant danger.

Daily life in a busy city street in the ancient Roman city of Pompeii.

Oil lamps were used to light homes.

25

Street Life

Roman cities were compact and the streets were lined with bakeries, greengrocers, taverns, butchers and every other kind of shop imaginable. In among the shops, hundreds of craftsmen plied their trades, blowing glass, shoeing horses, shaping pots and so on. The dirt, dust and din – and sometimes the stench – of daily life must often have been overwhelming.

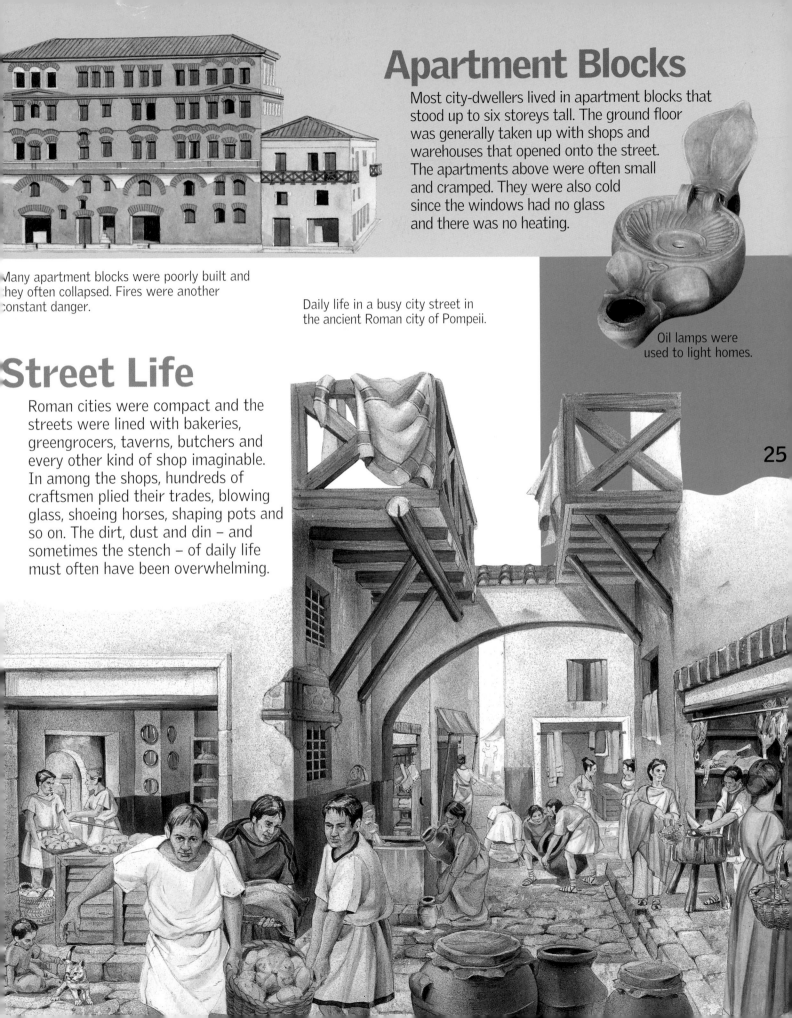

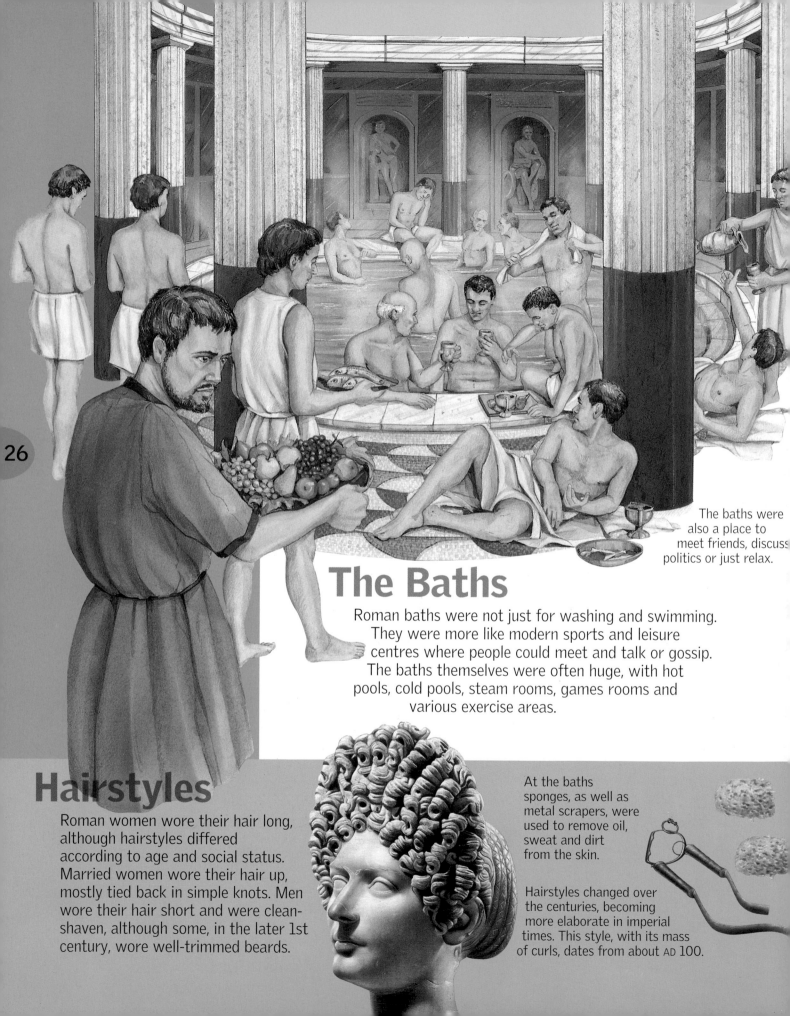

26

The baths were also a place to meet friends, discuss politics or just relax.

The Baths

Roman baths were not just for washing and swimming. They were more like modern sports and leisure centres where people could meet and talk or gossip. The baths themselves were often huge, with hot pools, cold pools, steam rooms, games rooms and various exercise areas.

Hairstyles

Roman women wore their hair long, although hairstyles differed according to age and social status. Married women wore their hair up, mostly tied back in simple knots. Men wore their hair short and were clean-shaven, although some, in the later 1st century, wore well-trimmed beards.

At the baths sponges, as well as metal scrapers, were used to remove oil, sweat and dirt from the skin.

Hairstyles changed over the centuries, becoming more elaborate in imperial times. This style, with its mass of curls, dates from about AD 100.

Perfume and Cosmetics

Perfume was popular and was made from plants and flowers, usually with the addition of oil. Cosmetics, which became popular in imperial times, were usually made at home using plants, insects and shellfish.

Women used polished mirrors, usually with decoration on the back, to apply cosmetics.

Body Care and Clothing

Body care was important to the ancient Romans. Every Roman town had public baths with separate areas for men and women. Most were free and many people went every day to exercise and bathe. Fashions changed over the 1,000 years of Roman history, although nowhere near as rapidly as they do today. Well-born people dressed elegantly and their clothing served to show their social status as well as to enhance their beauty.

Clothing

The tunic was the basic article of clothing for both men and women. Wealthier men wore longer tunics. Only free citizens (men) were allowed to wear the toga, a large, loosely draped garment, over their tunics. Women wore a long tunic tied high at the waist called a stola.

27

Jewellery

Wealthy women wore rings, necklaces, bracelets and pins. Talented local jewellers made beautiful items, but many of the rich often purchased fine gold jewellery with precious gems and diamonds imported from the Middle East and India.

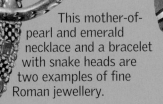

This mother-of-pearl and emerald necklace and a bracelet with snake heads are two examples of fine Roman jewellery.

A Roman woman wearing a cloak over her stola. Fabrics were made from linen or wool and could by dyed different colours.

Birth

The birth of a healthy baby was reason for celebration and ritual. Fathers raised their newborn children in the air, officially recognising and accepting the new baby into the family. Fathers could also choose to reject a child. Baby girls were named eight days after their birth, boys after nine.

During special ceremonies wealthy Roman children were given golden charms, like this one, to keep evil spirits away.

A Roman father acknowledges his child. Births were recorded at the Temple of Saturn.

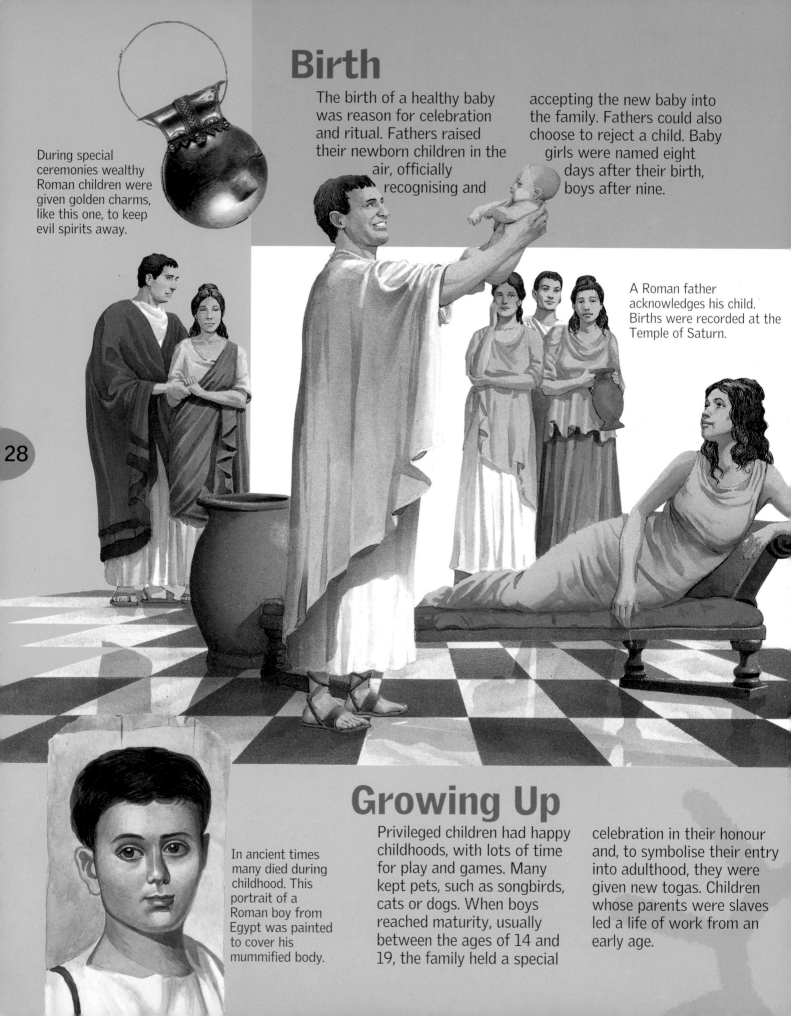

Growing Up

In ancient times many died during childhood. This portrait of a Roman boy from Egypt was painted to cover his mummified body.

Privileged children had happy childhoods, with lots of time for play and games. Many kept pets, such as songbirds, cats or dogs. When boys reached maturity, usually between the ages of 14 and 19, the family held a special celebration in their honour and, to symbolise their entry into adulthood, they were given new togas. Children whose parents were slaves led a life of work from an early age.

Marriage

Boys were thought old enough to be married at the age of 14 and girls at 12. Most marriages were arranged by the bride and groom's parents for social or economic reasons. After an informal written agreement was made, a betrothal ceremony was held with a banquet to follow. June was a favourite month for weddings. The bride was led to the groom's house in a joyful procession and was carried across the threshold.

During the wedding ceremony, performed by the matron of honour, the couple joined their right hands. A dowry was paid by the bride's father to the groom.

Families

Women in ancient Rome enjoyed more freedom than in many other early civilizations. Unlike Greek women, they could leave the house to shop, visit friends, attend dinner parties and go to public entertainments. Women enjoyed the same status as their husbands and were formally in charge of the household, directing the daily lives of children and slaves. When their husbands were away, Roman women often ran the family business.

Children in ancient Rome, much like children today, played with toys and games. This rag doll was found in a Roman city in Egypt.

Wealthy families hired teachers to educate their children at home.

Children learned to write using pens made from reed or metal and wooden tablets. Pens were dipped in ink made from soot.

Education

Not all children in Roman times went to school. Those lucky enough, almost always boys, started primary school at the age of seven where they learned reading and maths. A few went on to grammar school, where Greek and Latin grammar were taught. Only the sons of wealthy families continued their education and studied rhetoric, the art of public speaking and formal writing.

Different types of honey were produced in different parts of the Empire. The most popular kind came from Greece.

Farm Work

Life on the farm was hard work. Ancient farmers used animals to help them get things done. Farmers' carts and wagons, as well as farming machinery, were pulled by oxen. Donkeys were also used to do lighter work.

Oxen pulled a simple plough which broke up the top layer of soil to prepare the ground for seeds.

Farming

Crops

Cereals, such as wheat, barely, oats and rye, were grown to make bread, porridge-like soups and beer. Olives were an important crop as they provided fruit for eating and oil for cooking and for use in lamps.

By about AD 100, the fertile North African provinces were producing about 750,000 tons of wheat, most of which was exported north to Rome.

Although we know most about the many wealthy and powerful people who lived in the cities, it is important to remember that the vast majority of Romans lived in the countryside, earning their keep as peasant farmers and labourers. In early times, farms were mainly small, family-run places, but over the centuries many were bought up by larger estates. Well-off gentleman farmers had plenty of workers and slaves who did all the hard work.

Raising Animals

Farmers raised pigs, sheep and goats for their meat, wool and milk. Goat's and ewe's milk was made into tasty cheeses. Chickens and geese provided eggs and meat. Cattle were mainly kept as working animals and for the leather made from their hides. Animals were valuable property and many people, especially children and young people, worked as shepherds.

Pork was the favourite type of meat. Pigs were easy to take care of and were kept on farms all over the Empire.

This mosaic shows farmers at work – ploughing, sowing and taking care of vines.

arming methods did not hange greatly over the enturies. Before modern rm machinery was vented there was a t of hard and dreary ork to be done. risoners-of-war were ften forced to work s slaves on large states.

Grapes

Grapes were grown both to eat as fruit and for making wine, the Romans' favourite drink. The Romans learned how to cultivate vines from the Greeks living in southern Italy. The finest grapes were grown in Naples, near Mount Vesuvius, but vineyards were found all over the Empire, even in England.

Wine makers crushed grapes to a juicy pulp by stamping on them with their feet and heavy sticks.

Index